Hope

A COLLECTION OF POEMS

R. T. CHIWUTA

Illustrated by artspixels.com

Hope
A Collection of Poems

Copyright © 2024 by R.T. Chiwuta
Illustrated by artspixel.com

Paperback ISBN: 978-1-63812-888-5
Ebook ISBN: 978-1-63812-889-2

All rights reserved. No part in this book may be produced and transmitted in any form or by any means, electronic, or mechanical, including photocopying, recording, or by any information storage and retrieval system, without permission in writing from the copyright owner.

The views expressed in this work are solely those of the author and do not necessarily reflect the views of the publisher. It hereby disclaims any responsibility for them.

Published by Pen Culture Solutions   02/19/2024

Pen Culture Solutions
1-888-727-7204 (USA)
1-800-950-458 (Australia)
support@penculturesolutions.com

Hope
A Collection of Poems

I love you
I love you
Every time you speak
I become a better man
With every word
Every utterance
Like a gentle stream smoothing out a rough stone over time
Till its polished and perfect
As perfect as a stone can be
But it's not the stone
It's the stream
It's you
Your words too are nourishing
Like the water of the stream quenching life's thirst
Life's eternal thirst
You quench that thirst
Like a weary desert traveller finding a sacred oasis
I love you like one should love
Where love is a constant lesson
A constant lesson of how to be and let go
Let go of everything that's not you
And everything that's not us is hate and anger
Your love helps me find love, love and only more love
I love you
And love is hope
Love makes you hope for all the beauty of life to manifest in you life.

Introduction

I decided to title this book, hope and hope is characterised for me by the poem that has started us off. Hope, underpinned by love. Life, underpinned by love and us humanity like the rock, being constantly smoothed and made better by the soft continuous flow of love over us smoothing our rough edges. The rough edges of humanity. Hate and all the darkness we know. It seems at this time, humanity needs hope as it always has in many ways. The forces of division in every manner seem to be intensifying. Yet, when have they not been ever present?! Hence, onwards we march, and I hope the nourishing waters of love as in the poem can quench the thirst of the darkness that pervades over us and transmute it into a beautiful white light.

I dedicate this book to the
Hope of humanity.

Be motivated by love
Be inspired by love
Some people are motivated by hate
Inspired by hate
Strange people
Strange, strange people
How can you live to hate?
Go to sleep with hate in your heart and on your mind
Wake up with hate in your heart and on your mind
Spend the day hating
Plotting against those you hate
Strange people
Strange, Strange people.

Sweep hate aside
Sweep hate aside like the ash from a used up fire
Sweep hate aside like strewn rubbish after a wild gathering
Sweep hate aside like leaves all over your lawn during the autumn
Sweep hate aside from your heart
Sweep hate aside from your mind
Sweep hate aside from your heart so you can feel your connection to everyone else
Sweep hate aside from your mind so you can let go of the false hoods and untruths
Sweep hate aside so you can let go of the fear of those you feel threaten your sense of yourself
Sweep hate aside and make room for all
Sweep hate aside so you can experience just a sliver
A sliver of the peace and tranquillity of love and understanding
A sliver of what it is not to be so consumed by hate
It feels empowering
It feels fun when you are jeering, oppressing and bullying
But the true bliss of harmony escapes you
If only you knew how truly sad that is
Sweep your hate aside fascist, racist and all your other friends.

What a bunch of losers
You fascists and racists
Baying at football matches
Baying at foreigners
Baying
Baying
Baying with hate
Full of bile
Full of ill will
Listening to rhetoricians
Who wilfully mislead you
Wilfully instil hate in your heart
Not knowing these agents of chaos are as old as mankind
They are nothing new under this sun
Countless of them have come and gone
Telling you they care for you and are standing for you
But all their doing is teaching you to hate and facilitate their own ends
And you become a reflection of the hatred and imbalance in them
Don't listen to them
Instead take this thought
Have you ever really walked into your imagination?
Beyond your skin
Your geography
Your so-called place of birth
Walked deep into yourself
Within and without
Have you ever truly done that?

For then you would see
See the folly of your ways
When you know what we truly are
Within and without
Not what your lying rhetoricians tell you
And your racism and fascism tells you.

Old age
As the body succumbs to time, wear and tear
The bones creek
The clock goes tick tock
Time winds down
On your time on this journey of ours
Soon you will meet your maker
We are supposed to be wiser in our old age
But there's a saying that says
War is old men sending young men to die
So maybe we are not wiser
Some anyway
Some cultures honour old age
Your social status rises the older you get
Other more individualistic cultures might see the aged as a burden for they require care
Old age
Some fear
Fight against it
They sell us anti-ageing creams and the like
But don't you see the beauty of the wrinkles
The emerging white hairs
Acceptance
Being at the center
The middle of the beginning and the end
Transitioning from one state
One reality to another
Accepting the inevitable with grace and dignity
And if you have lived well
Then there are no regrets.

Xenophobia
That is the question
Maybe it's us idealists who are the problem
Trying to force everyone together
People want to look after their own as it were
Prioritise their own
Feel more comfortable with those who have the same traits as them
Same beliefs
Same modes of practice
Look like them
But the truth is that too is never a guarantee of peace
Most certainly not
And too what do we do with this jumbled up world we find ourselves in?
This interconnectivity
How do we live apart and live together?
How do we share
It's so interesting that when we are young
Our parents and elders implore us to share
But somehow when we get older it all gets lost
All the Holy books teach us about the values of sharing and caring but somehow it all gets lost
The highest philosophies and philosophers expound on the totality of things
But somehow it all gets lost
Politicians insist upon us their commitment to fairness, justice and their righthood
But somehow it all gets lost
Everyone is xenophobic

Everyone is racist
Or at the very least has the propensity to be
Europeans have borne the brunt of this label because they are the most recent pervasive conquerors and at present the most powerful nations on this planet
But look around the world
It's human nature to be xenophobic and racist
It's not an exclusive club
So, then the question is what then?
What next?
Do we prescribe our borders and everyone stay where they are?
The idea of nativism itself is flawed
What makes you a native of somewhere?
Time?
White Americans now call everyone foreign in a land that they are not native to seemingly
And shun immigrants
This America is just over two hundred years old
1776
Australia
1901
New Zealand
1840
Some of the other enclaves of white colonialism where nativism and xenophobia spout their ugly heads
That is infantile to the timescales of time
So, what's the timescale?

Ten years
Two hundred years
Five hundred years
A thousand
And human beings have always been and are nomadic
So, the nativists migrated from somewhere at some point
So, who belongs where really?
So much history
So much movement
Intermixing
In England they speak of Cheddar man
In Spain La brana man
Cheddar man a dark skinned hunter with blue eyes found in Somerset
The most quintessentially English sounding place
Dubbed the first Brit
La Brana man
A dark skinned hunter with blue eyes and dark skin
Along with Scandanavian and African DNA
I don't know how far you would get in a BNP pub full of golliwogs if you said the first Brit had dark skin
Or to racist Spanish football fans that the earliest inhabitants there were dark skinned
These claims made by so called main stream scientists
In main stream scientific journals and broadcast on the BBC and mainstream newspapers
Not purported by the brilliant Akala
Or some Afrocentric academic who can be written off for wanting to portray a pro black narrative

So, what do we do about it?
In any event the least I can say as a poet is hate is not the way
That's what I believe
The rest is up to individual reflection.

The point is
Open any page in history
Of this human race
It's the same thing
Killing and pillaging
Pointing fingers
At first they threw stones
Now it's laser guided missiles
Who knows what is next in the future
As the diabolical minds invent new weapons to kill
Chemical
Biological
I even heard something about sound waves
I don't care, who cares
So are those like me wishing for the impossible
Betting against nature
Betting against the sunrise
Betting against what's innate
Yet those who kill must come in their time and kill
And those who speak against it must come too and push back against them
Maybe that's the whole point of it.

We live at the edge of reason
Enoch Powell
There will be rivers of blood
Trump
Mexicans are rapists, thieves
Some South African politician who went viral not too long ago
Saying Zimbabweans must leave South Africa
His disdain to the extent that if he went into a hospital and there was a Zimbabwean baby on a ventilator
He would take it off for a South African
In South Africa
The former land of Apartheid
Where the whole conscientious world united for his sake one day not too long ago
A land where he had very little rights as a child and someone stood up for his rights
Yet today he is a man and diminishes the value of another
Today he speaks in the language and tone of the former oppressors
Life
The hostile environment
Theresa May
Priti Patel
Suella Braverman
Pushing a vitriolic and damaging campaign against migrants
Chipping away at people's humanity
For votes it seems

Or maybe it's their belief
Some kind of devaluing belief
Nigel Farage
These agents who exist to tear people apart
Cause rancour and discord
And they are manifold all over our planet
Anywhere you dare look
Question is
What happens when they go unchecked?
Unquestioned
Uninterrupted
Well, clearly they keep getting worse
Metastasise
First others are cockroaches
Then there is a institutionalised plan and system to exterminate them
As we saw in Germany
Genghis Khan is said to have killed at least eleven percent of the world's population during his time
His ideology clearly went unchecked
The decisions of these political and military leaders which kill so many
Many of whom we seem to venerate
Like Napoleon
Genghis himself
A man as complex as life itself
Caused the death of millions but said to be extremely loyal and generous to his followers
Caused so much suffering but vicariously brought so many closer together and into contact

Deified in some places

Castigated in others
A man who said about himself
That he was the punishment of God
For if humanity had not committed great sins
God would not have sent a punishment like him
Cities chose to surrender than fight his hordes for fear of their brutality
The Dichotic Dilemma
Yet more
Attila the Hun
Flagellum Dei
We look upon them with a sense of aggrandisement at times
Even a character like Winston Churchill
Instrumental as the history books say in galvanising England to rally against Hitler
Yet responsible for the Bengal famine and a colonialist
Tony Blair and George Bush's Iraq war and its destructive cost
In terms of human life and many other things
Despite your political position on the matter
We are talking here about the material consequence
The Vietnam war
The many bombs dropped still strewn over the landscape to this day
But that is humanity in the end I suppose
That is us
So maybe one shouldn't point fingers so much.

I must
I must
I must
Write an ode to all the musicians
The singers
Song writers
Those who play instruments
Of all kinds
Those who entertain us
With melody and rhyme
Rhythm
And use their appendages
Vocal chords
Lungs
And fuse with the Universe
As they channel inspiration
And hone skill
Mastered over long periods of time
Dedication and talent
Combining to create moments of bliss
For the rest of us
Maybe not so musically inclined
But get to enjoy the giving of the musician
The artistry
The singing
Oh the singing
How I love it
Like a soul singer
Or a country singer
Connecting with the deep wells of life's emotions

And telling the stories of our trials and tribulations
In life
In love
Poetry
Like the rapper
The conscious rapper
The truly talented ones
Weaving words seamlessly in the moment
Not written down
Not rehearsed
What skill
Music
The great deliverer
In all times
From the slaves in the plantations of the past
Picking cotton in the burning sun
Repressed and whipped
But finding solace in the humming, the hymns
And the singing

The so called Negro spirituals
It takes you away
Music
It does
Thank you Lord
Thank you for Music.

There is a song which says
It's been a long time coming
But a change is going to come
And Langston Hughes said in one of his poems
To not dream
Is to be like a bird with a broken wing
You cannot fly
So I dream of the most perfect world
Because as the song said
It's been a long time coming
But a change is going to come.

Hope
Hope
Hope always
The darkness will never win
It's pervasive
It's aggressive
But it'll never win
It's only as powerful as we allow it to be
To all the good people out there in the world
You are not alone
We are many

Racism
Tucker Carlson
Trump
Piers Morgan
CNN
Ben Shapiro
Bill Gates
Nigel Farage
China
Taiwan
Hong Kong
Russia
Ukraine
America
Nato
Palestine
Israel
Iran
North Korea
South Korea
Malema
ANC
Xenophobia
Honestly
Doesn't it sound just like noise now?
LGBTQ+
Immigration
Inflation
Rising cost of living
Climate crisis

Doesn't it just sound like noise?
Elon Musk
George Soros
Antipathy
Acrimony
Angst
Is this the Zenith?
Is this the Zenith of humanity?
What is the Zenith for humanity?
Human capacity
In all aspects
So, all this
All this noise
Is it some kind of lower vibrational frequency?
Some interference?
Some premeditated noise
To lower human kind's vibrational frequency
Human kind's perceptive frequency
Human kind's ability to tap into something higher
Something more divine
Than all that that's mentioned above
This noise
This numbing, buzzing
Traps humanity and keeps it at odds
At each other's throats
Figuratively and literally
It's impossible to imagine
That existence
Millions or even billions of years of evolution
And this is it?

What's reality to a stone?
Reality to a fish
Reality to a dog
Reality to a snail
We live in a field of everything
Every thingness
Imagine a stone is like a radio
But a stone is designed
Attuned like a radio to only pick up a certain aspect of that reality
Project a certain aspect of that reality
Live in that paradigm
For a stone
That reality is motionlessness
Being inanimate
Not sentient for all we know
For a radio it's to live
Live in the paradigm of sound that it is designed by us to exist in
However, both exist in the everything
The every thingness
So, the human
The sentience on this planet pick up the reality they pick up in the every thingness
The reality they are designed to pick up
Within the capacity of their mechanics
They are engineered beings
So, what does that mean then?
Well, it means everything exists right here
We are in it

We even are it
But we can only see what we can only see
Just like the stone
Just like the radio
Hence
Imagine if we had a quantum leap in perception
Somehow collectively tapped into the higher streams
The higher wavelengths of reality
The higher perceptions
Like the renaissance geniuses
And the theoretical geniuses who push things forward
Only this time it's tapping into a higher plain of humanity
For humanity
A higher plain of earth based consciousness
For we clearly live as asserted in a field of everything
And to some extent we do it already
We feel love
And we feel hate
But what if we tapped into something beyond that
Above that
New
Never before experienced in humanity
What would that mean for the next millennium?
For our progeny
For our perpetuity
What a fantastical poem
Well, I say imagine going to the twelve hundreds and telling them human beings flying in the air would be as common place as birds in the sky

So, we clearly have the capacity to tap into the impossible.

American bald Eagle
I saw you once
Not in your natural habitat
But in a zoo
Out in the open
But chained to the ground by a mighty chain
Sitting on a wooden stump
You seemed confused to me
Bemused
Looking around
Back and forth side to side
Like a captive would
A captive who knows they could otherwise be roaming the skies
Yet here you were
Those mighty wings unused
Chained to the ground
Something about this reminded me of the human zoos of the past
Which cause so much consternation
Sarah Baartman
And I thought
What true right have we to restrict your freedom for our entertainment
Just as the colonial Europeans then saw Africans as a lower species to marvel at in a zoo
Aren't we doing the same to you bald Eagle?
And all your fellow captives in the zoo
And yet some will say animals are not at the same level as human beings
We are a higher evolved species

Yet some will say we are all Earthlings
And so I pondered this American bald Eagle
All these ironies and conflicts
For you were an American bald Eagle
The Symbol of America
Freedom
Yet here you were chained
A sentient being
Yet your sentience is deemed below our own
Therefore, we can do to you as we please
And yet that's the hierarchy of existence to some extent
Predator and prey
The garden and the gardener who tends to it as they see fit
I contemplated all these things
With my children running merrily
Excitedly and haphazardly around me
Like free electrons
You chained so they
We
Could be entertained at the Zoo
On a cloudy but rather pleasant day
I was sad as I looked at you
And I didn't know what to do
For you looked lost
And I guess I too felt lost
For I didn't know what to do in that moment
So, I think I wished you well in my heart
Then I walked away.

Respect is the highest currency for humanity
I could write an expansive
Reflective
Discursive ode to emphasise this assertion
However sometimes
Brevity
Pithiness
Is more profound
So I will conclude as I began
Respect is the highest currency for humanity.

The irony of life is glory for one
Is abject misery and disappointment for another
Can be
Why did Arsenal have to bottle it again this season?
Said every Arsenal fan
And anyway
Man City have bought all their success
Lol
Laugh out loud as it were
The short hand and parlance of the day
But still so much to unpack there about reality
More so
 Why not write a fun and funny poem for a change
Three back to back draws
Gave away the title
Saliba
Why did you have to get injured
But as Big Sam said
City are good
Yes
Both their squads could win the Premier league
Bemused emoji
Guess I'm just a salty football
Haha
But well-done Arteta and the boys
David almost slayed Goliath
COYG
Onwards and upwards
Champions League next season
You're not defined but how you fall

But by how you get up
Come on you Gunners.
Hope.

What are we going to do about the killers?
Who hide in plain sight
For its impossible that African leaders don't care about their people
That there are no people in Africa who want to transform some of the negative conditions of
their people
Leaders in Latin America
And people everywhere who too care
It's impossible that Africa is somehow an automatic breeding ground for brutal dictators
But if you start to peel the layers of the rotten onion
Then the picture is laid bare
The puppet masters
The killers
Killers
Killers
Killers
Vile creatures
Vile
Vile
Creatures
Some speak of Karma
Some speak of hell
I personally don't know
I haven't seen it
But there must be some record
You think you go unseen here
You think your machinations crafty and validated
But I do believe in balance

Every action has a positive and equal reaction
And too I believe in transcendence
Such that the energy you put out will be addressed here or elsewhere
So maybe I do believe in Karma
I do believe in hell
But I'm a rationalist too
So, can't vouch for what I haven't seen myself
Or cannot prove
So, all you killers
The killers of Lumumba
The killers of JFK
The killers of all those who want to transform
It might seem wise here
You might get away with it in your dark shadows
And make your justifications
But I think there is probably a record somewhere
And one day in my youth when I saw the pattern of behaviour
The inevitable consequence for those who stood for what's right
I feared to raise my head above the parapet
In the realisation that they might kill me too

But as much as it hurts to say today
For I do love what I love
I will say it is what it is
To stand for what you believe in
Is to take a risk

So, they would rather us lie in the narrative of black incompetence
And so many believe it
But truth is they want the resources
That's all they ever wanted
Why invade in the first place
Carve up the whole continent
Travel perilous journeys over sea
Set up military bases
Who needs who?
Who needs who?
I want to say we need each other
As that is uniting
But today I woke up with the burning flame of indignation raging within me
For such much cruelty has been done
So much denigration
It must be at an END
Hope.

Today I burn with the rage of a thousand suns
Combusting all at once
All in close proximity
Producing the whitest most intense heat
Incandescent with rage at injustice
I burn with the rage of a thousand suns
In the hope for all that's good in the world
In the hope that total good can manifest itself
Like the great man once said
As was the popular refrain for those who were so down trodden
I am sick and tired of being sick and tired
We should all be sick and tired of being sick and tired
Where is the head of the snake
The slithering serpent causing darkness in the world
Once you Chop off it's head
The body will wriggle and writhe for a while
Then it's still and it cannot threaten anyone
Anymore.

Perhaps the greatest illusion for many
The greatest illusion of life
Is that this is THE life
That this life is it
And to win
Conquer
Succeed in this life is the most important thing
To dominate in this life
To accumulate in this life
To plunder
Not that there is anything wrong with some of those things
Like success
But what does it mean to be successful
Unfortunately, in our current world
It mostly means material gain
And of course there is nothing wrong with material gain itself
But
How, why and balance
Let's imagine that all death is
Is closing your eyes
And immediately opening your eyes in another reality
In an instant
And there as proposed by some faiths
You come face to face with the record of all your evils
All the harm you have wilfully done
With full insight
Full deliberation and the freedom of clear choice
Not the pressure of exigent circumstances

Choice
You chose to kill
Steal
Manipulate
Torture
Oppress
Lie
Wilfully
You chose this
Invest great time and effort in killing technology
It's only a question
Then imagine you had to face the consequences in some unimaginable ways
Let's propose that it's pain
As in true pain when you are present to the pain you caused others
The pain you feel when empathy, love, care, conscience and connectedness are present
Like the pain you would feel if you truly loved your child but somehow something you did caused it's death
As we know
So called evil people
Still love their children, family and loved ones in many cases
And you have to live in that pain for a time

For truly time is not real
It's just real here
The only real thing is eternity

So, God could prescribe that you live in that state till the balance is restored
Penance paid
If ever it can ever be
For to wilfully take, plunder destroy and oppress life
To deny another it's opportunity to be animate for your own ends
To kill its dreams
Which are endless
Is that something that can ever be repaid?
Imagine if that was the working philosophical position of most
If not all
What could be possible?
What would you do as an individual?
What would governments feel is justifiable?
Their secret services
Their secret programmes
Their clandestine activities
And every individual.

So that white lady in the jewellery shop
The shop attendant
Did she not make eye contact with me because I was black?
The attendant in the high-end shop
Were they nervous and suspicious of me because I was black?
Or was it me?
Was I the one who was nervous and suspicious?
Perhaps my fear of being thought of as a thief crippling me
My fear of completely losing it if they ever suggested it
Of course not violently because I'm a peaceful man
But losing it such that they would know I'm human
A good one I think
I hope
Without a shadow of a doubt
Quake them to their boots
History
Social conditioning
Paranoia
All colliding inside of me
The smear of black skin
How one black criminal is attributed to all
And not that their criminality is ever acceptable
Certainly not by me
But it's explainable
Wow you think too much
Just get in and buy the God damn ring

Or should I work so that more jewellery companies are owned and run by blacks so I never have to be paranoid ever again?
Oh, shut up.

You
Me
We
Love yourself
Not arrogance
But the acknowledgement that
I
We
Are a moment in space and time
Blessed to be formed in this existence as Me
As you
With a body allowing one to experience this phenomenon called life
Tres beautiful
Thank you
That which is.

As father and son gaze into each other's eyes
One just born
Only just working out what reality is
Whilst the other is middling out in age
And greying
What a sight for sore eyes
The transition of time
The father once a babe
Now a man
Eyes connected and souls intertwining with his new babe
Cosmic chemistry
Cosmic alchemy

As one slowly passes the baton to the other
You will be me son
I am you
And you are me.

18/5/2023

Welcome to the 4th dimension
From Duality to Reality
Words and ideas stumbled upon
Years before
In a haze and entanglement between realities
What does it mean?
What did it mean?
Utterances and declarations emanating from within and without
But what it all meant
Unknown to the rational mind
For this was beyond the rational mind
And when the rational mind took over
It was lost and confused by it all
Yet today an understanding has descended
And seems to go thusly
An intuitive knowledge and understanding
Acquired not from study
But a seeming apparition from the ether into the mind
And so it goes
First
Second
And third dimension existence is underpinned by duality
Duality being the fundamental factor of reality at this level
Let's call it the battle between light and dark
Good and evil
Polarities
Good and evil being God and the Devil

But outside of the frame of reference
Polarities just meaning opposites
And it's everywhere
Matter, antimatter
Acceleration, deceleration
Up, down
You get the point
So, anything is possible in this duality in the spectrum of good and evil
And phenomenologically with reference to polarities
So yes, in a Duality
In the first to 3rd dimension
Acts of extreme good and extreme evil are possible
Death is possible
Hatred is possible
Someone can abuse a baby
Kill a baby
Drop bombs on babies and children from drones and B57 bombers without batting an eyelid
All in a days work
And get medals and commendations at the end of it
Crush babies skulls in Cambodia
Baby P
Victoria Klimbie

Unmitigated evil
Which shocks the system
Only balanced out by the insistent good of those who exist to redress this
That's duality

Good and evil
All possible
And of course death
That very painful thing
Disastrous in this life
In the illusion of duality
The illusion of separation
In these lower dimensions
An illusion
However
Today my understanding caught up
Of the words I had written as I came out of the infirmary
The Dichotic Dilemma
The fabric of life
From Duality to Reality
The fourth Dimension
When the connection with the upper realms wore off
And I observed the words back then
What on earth is that!
And what does it mean?
And a quick Google search
Well, I'm clearly not crazy
All those thoughts I was experiencing and things I was writing about are referenced in spiritual teachings as old as man
Scientific ideas and social ideas which are verifiable
Duality is an observable phenomenon indeed
I'm not crazy
So, what's all this about?

And so, I discover
The fourth dimension is all about love
Did I read that somewhere or did I make it up?
Learn it somewhere
No Duality
No illusion of separation
Hence no death and no hate
Because when you know we are all one
You know nothing dies
When you know we are all one
Then you hate nothing
When all there is, is love
Pure love
Then all there is, is possibility
Contribution and service
See when you're living in duality
There is good and bad
And generally people want to get rid of bad things

Hence, why, people who do the most harm also think they are doing the most good
That's why politicians
Those divisive ones
Those demagogues make you hate others
Because they see them as bad
Then they make you see them as bad
Then we know what happens generally
Really, it's just duality at play
And when you become aware of it

It is so painfully obvious as to be liberating but frustrating
The Dichotic Dilemma
Until and unless you transcend duality yourself
Because being aware of it doesn't mean it's still not running you as you're still human too
So, the next thing then is to go outside of it
Move to the next dimension
The fourth dimension
Love
The collapse of duality
Dissolution
And oneness with all
Possibility and not logic
Logic is an exercise in duality
The interplay between what we think is possible and not possible
So, you're in a box
The box of human thinking
And we think that's intelligence
Yet all the true progress and genius is when we think outside the box
Outside what's supposedly logical
The imaginative leaps
That's why imaginative intelligence supersedes in terms of inventiveness all other forms of intelligence
So, the fourth dimension
Possibility
Love
Not logic

The world of the impossible
But in a good way only
For there is no duality
And so, imagine a world where we are all powered by love
And no hate for there isn't love's opposite
What would be possible?
We live a life of service
And success is a measure of how much you have served
For really it is in a way
As they say
If you want to be a millionaire
Serve a million people
But because there is no hatred or duality
Looking down
We are serving in ways that serve the self and serve others
Because we know we are all one

In universal love
And your success and actualisation is a by-product of how much love you've shown
And that's your legacy
Like Martin Luther King
His legacy was the love he showed for humanity
To the greatest extent
So, his words follow us today
Follow me
I don't know what philosophies ran him

But perhaps something akin to this lay in him
Because his words were visionary in truly divided times
Because to see the oneness of all and not be torn by a world that was so pulling for and run by duality
A viciously racist world
Is truly incredible
Knowing myself
That would've been a feat beyond me
So, I thank him for his vision
And on his enlightenment and shoulders I stand
So, the fourth dimension then
Love
Peace
Tranquillity
Not out there
But in here
In you
That's where the battle is
Because once it's won in here
Out there changes
And hence too who you are out there in the world and to others
The Dichotic Dilemma
The fabric of life
From Duality to reality
Welcome to the fourth dimension
Thank you God for allowing me to reach this day
For you know I almost took my life

Thank you for the love you have always surrounded me with in my life so I could sustain this path and painful enquiry

And thank you for the love you brought into my life so I could finally truly see

See conclusively that only love is the answer.

So, what does one do when the journey is done?
Reached the summit of the highest peak
Arduous preparation
Deliberation
Contemplation and stress
For the stress itself gives purpose to existence
But when you have overcome it all
Then what?
The irony of life
For the things that madden us
Actually give us purpose
And when they are gone
It's empty
So what to do
How do you create meaning
As we are programmed to create meaning by having something to overcome
Something to protect against something else
So, when you've answered all your questions that you wanted answered
What do you do?
Maybe you just go to bed
Grateful
Thank God
And wake up inspired
Maybe all there is then to do is enjoy this existence
Who would have thought that
What a thought
After all
There is music

Art
Sun rises
Friends
Family
The bird song
Waterfalls
Dancing
Laughter
Laughter
Laugher
Oh to laugh
A secret gateway
Into escapist moments
With each chuckle
To the crescendo and bliss of uncontrollable laughter
It was all here after all
The excitement of pursuing what you want
Or discovering what you want
What you're here for
Because you're here after all
The pursuit of being the expression of beauty

Not seeing it
For the senses can get overwhelmed
But being beauty
Does that compute I wonder?!

I was feeling sad and heavy hearted one day
When I thought I should have been feeling happy
So, I told my lover
And asked if she had any advice for me
Or what she thought
She asked
Oh, you have a heavy heart?
Well
Sometimes it happens
Allow yourself to go through the emotions
I always think that sometimes our souls remember things our minds would have forgotten kudhara
A long time ago
And I had known
But I knew again
That I had found a good friend in the moment
People can come into your life for a short time
Or a long time
Either way
Always make the most of it
Give as much as you can
Grow, grow, grow as fast as you can
Learn as fast as you can what they have to share
Laugh as much as you can
For each person
Is a moment in time
A window
A brief window into a different Universe
And infinite Universes
Infinite Universes that are not you

So
Each person is a treasure trove
When you always look for the value in the other.

So, what is human progress?
I say it is better to move slowly towards greatness
Than fast towards destruction.

I just saw a video
Sounded like a BBC journalist
You know these viral videos of today
And it showed an African Doctor in colonial Africa
Performing a craniotomy in the Village
To his credit the BBC journalist sounded fascinated
And he was platitudinous
But alas he could only describe this Doctor as a witch Doctor
For, of course this clear display of knowledge not just of the human body
But of surgery, chemistry and everything else
Could only be explained by some mysticism
Not that this man was intelligent and knowledgeable
For, he was just but an African savage in the jungle
Deepest darkest Africa
What do they know?
It's a continent with no history and no enlightenment to offer the world
The dark continent
Alas
What have we gained?
And what have we lost?
Us Africans
We certainly have lost a lot
Victor Orban
The controversial Hungarian President
When Ukraine was invaded by Russia and they welcomed in Ukrainian refugees
His comment was

At least these refugees are educated
Not like the ones we are used to
These darkies
It's staggering at times how some Europeans operate with a distinct selective historical outlook
It's of course deliberate in many ways
In any event
The sense of European supremacy is as common place as breathing in this epoch
So, to lament it seems a waste of time
So, the question is then
How long will we keep looking down on each other?
This African Scientist
Performing a craniotomy
Without the plethora and menagerie of western surgical equipment
Safely
Where the patient is able to walk straight after the surgery
Not anaesthetised
Clearly having been given some cocktail of plant medicine
Again, outlining great knowledge of flora and fauna
And our biological and existential connection to the earth
One of the most complex surgeries
Where a misstep can have irreversible consequences
What have we lost?
What have we lost?

What is it about ourselves?
About Africa that they want to remain lost
They must deride?
Deride and deride?
Oppress and oppress?
Yet this book is titled Hope
So, I'm highlighting the inaccuracy of the portrayal of a people
One hopes for an eternal transformation in their state and condition.
The state and condition of humanity.

I want
When I'm done
When they lay me in the ground
Or they burn this body to ash
This astral vessel
When my energetic signal transmutes
I want
I want to leave a world
I want to leave the world
Leave a message in the world
The possibility in the world
If not now
One day
The racist
The xenophobe
The misogynist
The killers
The oppressors
And all those people
Can be looked at as a relic
A relic of fascination
Like the dinosaur
As in
Wow
Those creatures once existed
People used to think like that
How fascinating
How wondrous
Hope
Overpowering hope.

Something happens in the space
When authentic love is present
Is this true or not?
Have we not all experienced it?
When real love is there
Is it not something truly fascinating?
Something completely better than hate
As they say
Jus sayin
Well I am just saying
Hope.

When you hear these ex-military combatants speak
Especially when listening to a former serving American soldier
That matters little though
Point is they talk of confirmed kills
As though your confirmed kills are something to be proud of
Am I an alien?
Why do I find this so bizarre?
Who could proudly declare this?
Pronounce this to the world?
Go on podcasts
Interviews
Pronounce it in movies
What don't I get about human existence that this baffles me?
Yes
He's a soldier
They are soldiers
Killing is their job
I must be an alien
I'm not from here
It just doesn't sit well with me
If I did have these kills because I was a soldier somehow
I wouldn't want to tell anyone
I certainly wouldn't want to sit in the glory of it
And I pray to the heavens
All the Gods of all the Universes that the dark unwinding of fate doesn't ever find me having no choice but to be a soldier

Yes, I am an alien
And I'm fine with that
Hope.

Money
Money
Money
Money
Money
It makes the world go round they say
Imagine being given free will
Then inventing something that entraps us all
Enslaves us to pursue it
So much so that we would propose that the great forces that support our earth
Are attributed to it
It's only a saying someone yells
To highlight the centrality of the exchange of money to our existence
Well, what of those without it?
Is it optimal?
Is this the highest possibility of exchange?
We know what the reckless pursuit of it can and does do
Money
Money
Money
Money
Money
Hope
Hope and imagination this time.

So, one is watching Good Will Hunting
Let's call that one
A poet
A dreamer
Or one just watching a movie
One of the best movies ever made
So, what does one see
One sees Will
A diamond in the rough
Literally and in his mind
Tortured by life
Impoverished by life
Yet he's genius outstrips learned professors
An everyday ruffian
In the film they talk of Ramanujan
A real life diamond in the rough
Who by apparent coincidence found a text book of mathematics
Yet with no formal training
Profoundly changed the path of mathematical enquiry in a meaningful way
Came up with and solved problems thought of as unsolvable
Will easily outstrips all the privileged Havard pupils
But of course they've done nothing wrong
I'm not a classist
Fighting a class war
You can't be blamed for having parents who aspire for the best for you
Or circumstances which favour you

Yet the point then is
How many Wills are out there
Of course he is fictional
But Ramanujan was real
How many geniuses are trapped in favelas
And Kibera
The slums of Calcutta
And townships of Soweto and everywhere else
What of human potential if we harnessed the power
of all that we can be
Give every child
Every opportunity to reach their potential
Discover it
What becomes of human existence?
What would we need to remodel?
Redefine
Hope.

As we've already established
A few poems back
I am an alien
Or at least I realised I must be
As I was finding myself bewildered
And befuddled
By human blood lust
So, it became apparent upon further thinking
Enquiry
As one does
In the flow of the day
That oh my
The fixation is a fear of death
Ultimately
We want the things that we are fighting for to survive
Whether it's ourselves
Or some idea
Etcetera
Hence its clear
Who are, and who have been the most dangerous people on this earth?
The people who fear something dying
A race
A way of life
A belief
Their point of view
Their dreams
And such and such
And of course to completely escape the fear of death
One must disconnect from attachment

But isn't to be attached to be human?
So, the question is
Can you just love without attachment?
Then the point is
Back to the point
Imagine if instead we didn't live in fear of death
Because its guaranteed
For all
Things die
It is an absolute certainty
So, hence
Instead of fighting death
Why don't we embrace life
In the understanding and expectancy of death
In the understanding of change and evolution
Change is death
Evolution is death
Because the preceding thing is superseded by the pursuant thing
But then also its to really see
The transitory nature of this life

Which leads me again to the assertion
I must be an alien
I never understood people's obsession with life
And fear of death
The Universe is infinite
In this life you have between zero to no more than a hundred years generally to live
And people
Energy just transmutes
It doesn't perish
Ask all the physicists
So, we don't die
We change state
The spiritualists will confirm this too
So, what's a better obsession for humanity
Being fixated on not dying
And the narrow things we value not dying
Or being obsessed with making this life extraordinary for everyone who incarnates here
Hope.

Love is the elixir of life
It cures all the poisons
Spiritual
Physical
Mental
For if you are loved
And there is love
It's better
It's easier
Yes, there is everything to contend with
And a lot we must do
But if love is present
Then all else is better
So, it is the elixir of life
Love is the elixir of life
And we won't find it in a chemistry bottle
We will find it in our hearts
In all our hearts.

What is hope after all?
Hope is that thing
That inscrutable thing
Inscrutable in that it keeps us going when logic has failed
Logic tells us
There's no way out
There are no other options
I am at rock bottom
Things will never change
This is the worst of it
How can I ever come out of this
Logic tells us that
Yet hope says yes there will be a way
Yet we are taught to rely so much on logic
Such a limited thing
To think within the confines of what you think is possible
When hope exists in everything that seems impossible
Hope exists outside we think is possile
It is exponential, limitless, adroit and designed to blast through any fortification of human limitation
Things you can't even imagine
Things you don't even know
Possibilities you didn't even know were possible
That's hope to logic
So, what is hope?
Hope says we can overcome anything
Hope says all will be well
Hope says persevere

Look for solutions
Sway and sway away from the naysayers
The doomsdayers
The only doom is the doom of a lack of hope
Those who try and convince us of the darkness of things
The dark only exists to usher in the light
The dark only exists to give us rest from the chores of the day
The dark is a companion of the light
Not antithetical
But symbiotic and synergistic
One arises from the other
As the other comes
The other goes
If it were to ever stop
All here would be over
The dark gives us a chance to rest from the troubles of the day
So we can wake up recharged to face the following challenges of the next day
So those who don't see that the challenges of the day
Are a call to hope
To togetherness
Not fear mongering
Don't know of the true meaning of things

We suffer not because life is hard
Yes, life is hard and is a challenge

But we suffer when we stop believing in solutions and abandon hope
Solutions that bind and build
Create new possibilities
Instil hope not fear
Speak of possibility not catastrophe
How many have predicted the end of the world?
Say we are over populated
What narrow vision
We are not over populated
We are just poor managers
We are wasting our resources
Those who speak of over population
Are like a doctor wanting to amputate a leg because a patient is obese
I couldn't find a better analogy
It's 1 AM in the morning
I should be sleeping
Point being
The leg is fine
Clearly there are many other problems
Actually, the analogy fits perfectly
So, if the patient is obese
We could say there are issues of over consumption
Gluttony
Greed
The leg is culling the numbers
Reducing the size of the body
But that doesn't solve the actual problem
Which is the lifestyle

Poor management
Poor way of life
Poor values
So, to all those who say we are over populated
We can reframe this certainly
And most importantly
Are you spreading hope or panic
Are you inspiring meaningful solutions
Or inspiring some quite malignant propositions
Hope
Hope is so many things
Humanity is littered with examples of the triumph of hope
It's worth more than everything else we treasure
Hope is the currency of love
Love's motivation
Love's active ingredient
Hope is the possibility of things that can truly dazzle us
It far outstrips
And outweighs anything else I can imagine
Any other human quality

Hope
Love
Bravery
Courage
The most noble human traits
Honesty
That too

But I digress
Hope
Life's Imaginarium
The source of possibilities outside of the imagination
The creative factor
The X factor to existence
An engine for life and persistence
So, with that established
What is the possibility for humanity if we hoped for a peaceful and loving world?
Achieved it
Then hoped for more and more things
That we can't even imagine right now
Because we spend so much time doing everything that we are doing right now
Which I've spoken about ad nauseum
In every book I've written
Yes, this piece is very first person
The thing is
When you are present to the possibility of the Universe
When you have been touched by an awareness outside of the everyday
Which I will say I have
But even from a young age when you have had a critical way of observing reality
Some things seem really bizarre and asinine
How can people not see that?
How can people not get that?
How can people believe that?
Shona people don't like Ndebele people or visa versa

Xenophobia
Racism
War
Etcetera
Hatred
I mean I'm human too
So, I've had to unlearn some of these things
Particularly Racism
Which has been a tough one to unlearn
In a world built on Racism
Tribalism was an easy one to unlearn because my dad is Shona and my mum is Ndebele
Xenophobia
I've never been particularly nationalistic
Maybe just a God given endowment
More seen the world as one
So again, an easy one to tick off

War
Well, we wouldn't have been liberated from colonialism without fighting a war
But I don't get killing
So, I easily unlearned that
I learnt to value life very early on
Again
Maybe just an endowment from God
So, I suppose, yes
How do I get to this somewhat fervent position?
Where I'm on my fourth book
Pretty much saying the same thing in different ways
Well, I suppose
I hated life for so long because I immediately connected with all that was negative about it
And boy it's a lot
Nuclear war
Just the thought
The culmination of all human malice and failings
Yet ironically
Human brilliance too
So yes
For the many evils of life
I hated life
But then I had children
And my God do I have to change this place for them now
No excuses
Yet in the process, wow
What a world it would be if all children were safe

At least safe from the things we can control
And we strive to make life exceptional
Imagine the quantum leap it would need to be in what human beings are
In what humanity is
That's hope.

Don't beat your kids
Your children
You don't have to
You never have to
As an adult
You are incensed by another adult assaulting you
Even poking your forehead
Or bumping into you
What then of a fully grown adult
Letting their full might
Reign on a child
A tiny defenceless child
It is abominable
Imagine the world you are creating
For that child
For what they believe about the world
Yes the Bible said he who spares the rod hates his son
But he who loves him is diligent to discipline him
And most people especially Christians commit to this parental maxim based on that
However, what I will contend is that as in the Bible
A lot can and is down to interpretation
And what I interpret there is the emphasis on discipline
And discipline can be attained in so many ways outside of performing violence on defenceless children
You are enforcing violence as an agreeable position
As a meaningful and just way to install and instil what you want in others
Hence, the world we live in some ways
If your own parents can beat your mercilessly

What is stopping you from beating your fellow pupil at school?
And we call it bullying
It's just mimicking
Who else uses violence?
Take your pick
The who's who of the nasties of the world
Just yesterday I learnt
The difference between utilitarianism and deontology
Maybe this is why
For this poem
You can create a beautiful strong responsible brave courageous human being
With communication and love
Do we want the same world
Or a new world
The old world or a new world
Discipline doesn't mean beating
It means structure
Commitment
Consistency and love
Does the outcome matter despite how we got there?
Or is there criminality in the action despite the outcome irrelevant?

I say don't beat your children
Love them
Let's try that and see what world they create
Don't shout at them or belittle them
You scar them
Encourage them and raise them
Grow them
And let them know its a great thing they were born
When you scream and shout and they don't listen and the whole place seems to be crumbling
As they run around everywhere
Yes, it can be challenging but guess what
But life is challenging and all of that is a reflection of you
It's a reflection of your internal state
If they are running around and you see chaos
It's because you are in a chaotic mind state
If they run and around and you see that they are playing
Then you are in control
And if they start to get out of control
You take control and restore the equilibrium of the situation
You nurture, you parent
And the better you are at doing that, the better you are as a person
And the better you are at managing your own life and emotions
The authority you have over them with your word

Is a reflection of the authority you have over yourself with your word
And if you have true power
And your voice speaks, even gently
They will hear you profoundly
Especially when the instruction echoes from the deepest wells of your love and they know you love them
Everything is an upward lesson to eternity.

All of it
Is truly amazing
Spectacularly amazing.

God really doesn't let anyone or anything suffer
I'm compelled to say this
And to observe existence
It seems preposterous to say
Preposterous to propose
Insane
Maybe
Even
But imagine
If it was possible
That really
God doesn't let anyone suffer
Anything suffer
What an elaborate trick
What a truly intricate ruse
Imagine if it were possible
What a truly amazing act of magic
This life
I'm only saying imagine
Just try it
Like it was a thought exercise
A thought exercise
Not a postulate of reality
A thought exercise
Imagine as far as you can
With this brain
How amazing would that be?
And what could it mean
Just a thought exercise.

What do you do in a scenario where everything doesn't work?
Everything seems to be not working
Well
You do something.

I once asked an elder
How do we transform Africa?
How do we transform our country?
How do you turn around a situation that seems impossible to remedy?
As I was being weighed down by the ignominy and pain of this colonial mess we inherited
The world even
And he said well, my young mind
In my experience at the top
For he had held high position
It's actually not that hard
All you need to do is change the culture at the top
That's it
It's easier than you think
I went instantly from being hopeless and despondent
To being certainly more hopeful
And I see now without knowing
That, that moment
That hope was quite defining
I hadn't even known
Thank you elder
And that's why in African culture
The older you are
Doesn't mean you are becoming less useful
You grow more in value
At least to say you're not seen as a burden to society to be looked after
More a wise guide
A revered soul that has walked the longer path ahead
It is good.

So, Tina Turner died today
Brutalised and vandalised by her ex husband
Left with nothing
In fact escaped with nothing
Ran from him
In the dead of night
To a fate she couldn't predict
Clad only with the courage in her heart
To overcome the unforgiving demands of a male dominated industry
Given two weeks to make an album
The result then being the album going five times platinum
Hence, becoming a Rockstar at forty two
Restarted her whole existence
At a time when most are giving up on theirs
A black middle aged female rock and roll star
Headlining with the rolling stones
A pop icon
Hope
Courage
Strength
The most remarkable of stories
And a microcosm of potential human transformation
A woman brutalised by her black husband
Who found true love in a white Swiss man
Such that when she was at death's door
With her body failing
Her kidneys
And was ready to have her life taken away

Assisted suicide
He could not bear it
He could not imagine another life
Or being with another woman
Even though he was sixteen years her junior
And could potentially have any woman he wanted
He gave her his own kidney
So, she could live longer
And he could be with her just a bit longer on this earth
A white man
A black woman
Love
True love clearly
Demonstrably
So maybe racism is already dead
Or maybe today it dies for me
Or does it just live in those who allow it to live in them
But then you only need a few of them and spoil the whole show
In any event
Tina Turner
Courage

Strength
Power
Hope
Talent
Expression
Entertained us
Gifted us her soul's expression

It's only when the story is told
We discover what a human being can truly be
Rest in peace.

Hashtag
National shutdown said the flier
South Africa is full
We are no longer supporting illegal foreigners
Then in red and capital letters
DO OR DIE FOR YOUR COUNTRY
Then in went on to say
To all foreigners in South Africa
Deadline to leave South Africa
Is 01 June 2023
Venue
Union building
Date 01 2023
Time 08:00am
It was never about race
It was never about skin colour
The ignorance of mankind
They could be doing so many other things.

If you only see a positive world
Saw a positive world
Then only a positive world exists
If you only see
Saw a negative world then a negative world exists
Imagine if we all see
Or Saw a positive world
What would be our attitude to others?
To problem solving
Would we even believe in problems?
For if everything was positive
Then we wouldn't believe in problems
See problems
Maybe our whole language would change
Perspective
A problem becomes a challenge
Or maybe even an opportunity
An exercise
A learning point
An opportunity to excel
Achieve
Work together
Or anything else
As opposed to a problem
Something burdening
It would be something inspiring
Inspiring you to be the best you
That's a shift
A quantum shift

We already know anyway what it looks like when people see a negative world.

Compassion
Empathy
Love
The triumvirate
Maybe even the elixir
The Panacea.

Perpetuity.

The triumph
Is found in the adversity
The story
Is found in the adversity
You can only overcome
If there's something to overcome
So then that's life
Not that it's a ruse
Maybe it is
By some devilish God
A trickster God
Or maybe a plain to be
Who knows
Who cares
But the reality is adversity exists
And all the courage
The tales of courage
And the wisdom to be found
The intelligence
Will and determination
The fortitude
All come from there being adversity
The hope for better times
Comes from being in times of adversity
So, it's not that you won't find adversity
That's a certainty
It's what you will find out about yourself
So today I saw a young boy from South Africa
Who lost his leg as a child to cancer
An amputee with one leg

I saw him dancing on a television stage in England
To an audience of white faces
Hoping only the best for him
And he danced like an angel
On only one leg
You could have never imagined it being possible
Not to this level of execution
Not to this level of beauty
The most elegant and exquisite expression of humanity
In movement
Courage
Strength
And artistic expression
They've said it over the ages
It's not the size of the problem
It's the size of the courage inside of you to face the problem
Oh my
Oh my
It's stunningly beautiful
And when he was done

Everyone was moved
Beyond anything they could have ever imagined
I think the whole Universe was moved
And he was beautiful
Reflecting the beauty of it all.

I have just realised why I write
I write not for the betterment of blacks
As I once thought
Their emancipation from oppression
In all its forms
As it has manifested in our life time
I write not for the betterment of the human race
As I once thought
For who am I to suppose how other humans should behave
Their beliefs and all this
And who am I to possibly think I can emancipate the human race from its collective ignorance
Hubris
Delusion of grandeur
Pathology
However
I have realised today
With thanks and deepest gratitude
That I write for the betterment of the human condition
For this incorporates all it is to be us here
Not just a race
For we live with everything else that's here
The rocks
The bacteria
The water
The viruses
The animals
The plants
The weather

And all else I could mention
Seen and unseen
Known unknown and yet to be known
The human condition is a galvanising phenomenon
Of all things
And ultimately it's for this I write
The improvement of everything
Just slowly
Incrementally
And if I can move the evolutionary needle by an unnoticeable minuscule micron
Then I would have lived my purpose
The best life I could have lived
And if I can just evolve myself
Perhaps that certainly will be the greatest triumph
Perhaps that's all I'm here to do.

Chakanaka
Chakanaka
Okuhle
Kuhle
What's beautiful
Is beautiful
All is beautiful
Amen.

The ISS is off
Into space
As some lumbered
Some built a station for humanity in space
A new dawn
A new day
A signal for so much
As humanity went into orbit
Breached the unseen forces that keep us bound to the ground
What is to come I wonder?

When you are a child
They tell you a second is the smallest unit of time
And most will go throughout life with this frame of reference
Our clocks
Watches
And lives are run largely
By the seconds
Minutes
And hours
Of course there is the millisecond
And microsecond
Then one day you discover
There is a nanosecond
And think
Oh my
That's another layer of reality
Then you live and think that's all there is
Because nano means one billionth of a metre
I mean a billionth
Only to then one day find out
There is a picosecond
Which is one trillionth of a second
Surely
This is getting ridiculous
How do you even measure that?
Then a femtosecond
One quadrillionth of a second
Now we are just making up words
Attosecond

Zeptosecond
Yoctosecond
Rintosecond
Quectosecond, one nonillionth of a second
If you would believe that
Makes no sense to the common man
So, what is reality really?
What is anything?
What is all this to the starving child?
Or the marriage breaking down?
Or humanity?
Or anything really?
Then I see there is Planck time
Right at our limit of capacity it seems
Presumed to be the shortest theoretically measurable time interval
Imagine if we humans can do this
Yoctoseconds
Rintoseconds
Quantum mechanics
Then

What can God do?
Even a minor Deity
Yes, we are minor Deities too
As expressed above
We too can manipulate
Invent and understand
Animate
Imagine

Spawn
Bound by gravity
And yet we are so feeble
In feeble bodies
So prone to compromise
Of all manner
Our life span so short as to be meaningless
Relative of course
A minor Deity indeed
Yet we are this
Planck time etcetera
So, what of the greater Deities?
Greater than us
And perhaps even the Deity
The original
Ground zero
Alpha and Omega
Everything and nothing
Light and dark
The one
The one and only
What of that mighty almighty thing
The almighty one
I tremble
Not in fear
But in obsequious admiration
Not obsequious because this God demands it
But obsequious because I am dazzled at the magnificence of this thing

That my feeble mind can only run around in dazed admiration and a willingness to serve
So maybe just a drop of this divinity can land on me
Because anymore
In this feeble body
Surely means death
Of the mind
Maybe even the physical body.

Sometimes the thing that makes you the strongest
Is the thing that makes you the weakest
It has been said
It's what allows you to conquer
And yet makes you most vulnerable
And ultimately blinds you
Binds you to a fate
And a way of being
So, what to do
Well
Evolve
Learn from the past
Else you are a fool
As harsh as that sounds
The imperative of our life here is survival
Existence
Evolution
Adaptation
That's the surest way to survive
Exist through all that changes and threatens.

Thought
As I listen to Salif Keita
Kuma
Instantly haunted
Entranced and transported
As one who has been educated as a European
And now lived in Europe
I now perhaps feel as the Europeans felt
Of course some derided us
Us Africans
But I do not
But I do though feel as they did
As I listen to this song
This great sense of mystery
And wonder
The same way they describe African mysticism
African culture
With bewilderment
Inquisitive intrigue
Like there is something deeply mysterious here
Can't quite put my finger on it
Maybe something ancient
Maybe even something knowing
But they would dare not admit that to themselves
For it would have disastrous implications to their economic models
And the ideas they developed to justify a lot of their positions
Like the tales you hear of the Dogon
The Hadza

I am transported straight there with this song
Salif Keita
This albino man
This African man
Music genius
Blending Africa and the West
Evolving
Adapting
With a voice that will rouse the spirit
Maybe that's why I am alive
To hear Salif Keita's voice.

Some pursue happiness through hatred
For when they hate
It's in the pursuit of happiness
A world without those they see as the problem
Some pursue happiness through hard work
Persistence
They pursue happiness through pursuing money
Riches
Which is fine
I could go on
But I will say
In this moment I realise that firstly
At least I
Should pursue happiness
Through love and peace
Not something I must find
Something I must indefatigably work for
Through finding a partner
And all the other things that might make me happy
A hobby
But rather by just being love and peace
And being at peace
And in love
In love with it all.

There is so much suffering here
So much pain
That you must choose hope
Only hope
Hope always
Hope
Hope and kindness.

It's so clear to me
Clear as day
As the clearest
Crisp
Sunlit day
That if there was peace and love in the world
A golden age would dawn
To dwarf the human progress of the last hundred years
Such that if humanity is amazed by the last hundred or so years
It would be blown away by the ensuing hundred
Because it would be wilfully creating
With Love and possibility
Not reacting
To the impact of missteps
Misguidance
Barbarism and insanity
Humanity has a clear choice
Do we want to be lead by the monsters in us?
The monster in us
Or the creative Saint
The genius
The inspired architect.

How funny is love
When you shout because you love each other
Fight
Not physical fighting of course
That's for the dull and uninspired
Because everything can be resolved in communication
Even strong
Forceful communication
That's love
Violence is not love
It's control
But how funny is love
When you shout because you love each other
Fight
And when it's resolved
How good it feels
Majestic
That's what peace feels like
That calm serene space
To build something new
As long as you don't go back
But use that space to go forward
Never back
Always forward
Closer and closer
That's real love in action
When you shout
Because you love
Fight
Not physical fighting

Because physical fighting in this case is for brigands
Just like all war
Ultimately.

My heart was sad
Now it rejoices
The mind was resolute
But without the heart
Gently guiding the way
The mind gets lost
In the confusion of things
The heart is like a magnetic pole
Guides the mind on where best to go in this strange world of ours
And without a heart
A good heart
You can get irrevocably lost
So, my heart was sad
For it had lost its compass
But now the heart rejoices
And the mind knows where to go
Hope.

Today
I know what a soulmate is
For my soul was surely shattered
A soulmate completes something that's already whole
Adds
A soulmate makes something that's strong
Even stronger
Perhaps impregnable
But oh my
To lose your soulmate
I don't want to lose you
Not just yet.

Today I verily know I'm not just flesh
But I'm spirit too
And what is flesh?
Yet it is
More so
Spirit is more
So much more
To limits beyond limits
To imagination beyond imagination
To possibility beyond possibility.

Today I saw a man
On this thing that connects us all
This thing we call the Internet
Optic cables
Wi-Fi signals and everything else
He was a white man
A white man in Zimbabwe
His circumstances
The irony of ironies
The Dichotic Dilemma
Humanity
And what is us
This man seemed to be the worst victim of circumstances
Impoverished and unemployment
A white man
Seeking and having found refuge amongst the blacks
The blacks who not too long ago would have
been societally beneath him by law and political design
A white man who had married a black woman
In Zimbabwe
Something that gets you shunned by the Rhodies
The white Zimbabweans
His fellow white Zimbabweans
He had sired a child with this lady
But lost them both in a cyclone
Cyclone Idai
A man ravaged by nature itself
And the complex interweaving of existence

As I observed him
Being interviewed by a black journalist
A man so poor
A white man so poor
Something I never imagined was possible growing up in Zimbabwe
A white man in a level of destitution I only saw
Ironically when I came to the West and saw homeless white people
His home for over a year
Was an old ramshackle rusted car
Given to him by his black mechanic friends in the mechanic yard for him to reside in
Asked how he had fallen so low
He explained he had lost his job when his employer died
The business was taken over by his wife
Who sacked him because she was pressured by her family
Why do you employ a white man when we have no jobs they asked?
Asked where his family was
He responded in his thick Shona accent
That he was raised as an orphan
Asked whether he had sought help from his white affluent community
He said they told him to go back to his black people
Yes

Those are Rhodies

Yes that's racism
Yes
That's what happens when you've been taught to hate
Raised on hate
Such a thing doesn't surprise the journalist
No shock on his face at all
It's to be expected as the rising sun
The opposite would actually have been the miracle
For we know the Rhodie
After all
They are eponymously named after Cecil John Rhodes himself
Coloniser extraordinaire
A toxic inheritance
To this day
Black is black
And white is white
In the former Rhodesia
Now back to the man
I juxtaposed his existence and mine
Nestled here in the West
In Europe
In the very bosom of his ancestors
The United Kingdom
Benefitting from Western privilege
An author
A professional
Even an English man
Whilst he ironically is a Zimbabwean
His shona better than mine

My English better than his
So, what is humanity?
He had mixed race children
I have mixed race children
And I wonder what the Rhodie would think of that?
I dare you to speak ill off my children Rhodie
Not that I am a man of violence
I am a man of peace
So, I dare you to allow hate to fester even further in you
Your choice
After all
It's your God given right
As your ancestors taught you
It was your God given right to rule over the black
I imagine that's still how you justify your feelings and thoughts today
How to live as a blind man who thinks he sees all
So back to this man
This poor, poor man
This emblem of what it truly is to be human
Opportunity and circumstance

Everything else is a created myth
Power grabbing
Yet the irony is the humanity he was being shown
Even in the dreaded comments section
That very 21st century thing
You would have thought the black Zimbabweans would be rejoicing at this

A sort of schadenfreude
How the great white man has fallen
But no
They expressed pity for the man
Lamented the ruination of a nation
That caught even a white man in it's ravages
I declare that the black race have fought their oppression whilst displaying the highest attributes of what it is to be human
And at times an incredible capacity to forgive
Ian Smith
The former President of Rhodesia
Who profusely hated the black
Was able to live out his life in peace after independence
No one accosted or threatened his life
And so he died in peace on his farm
So, what of it all?
In this rambling yarn
I say this
We are all human
The colonialists taught white superiority
And I believed it
But when I moved to the West with my education
I didn't find the intellectual superiority
When I became a professional
I had white assistants
A lot of the cleaners were white
I had the expert knowledge
My analytical mind marvelled at this
So, it wasn't true

And yet I learned not to judge them
Or rejoice that I was supposedly not inferior
Or even better than them
I realised they are human just like me
I realised they are just people trying to look after their families
Trying to live their lives
Then I contemplated it all
I contemplated it all
I contemplated it all
Then one day maybe I will see
That, that's the greatest lesson.

Find yourself a partner who believes in you more than you believe in yourself
Who sees you greater than you can even imagine yourself
That's someone who truly loves you
That's someone who will say the right things when you need to hear it
Guide you the right way when you're getting lost
Stand for you
Protect you
Even from yourself
Encourage you even more than your family
Your friends
Someone who makes you feel as wide as the expanse of the universe
As tall as the length of the tallest imaginable thing
That's the person to be with
Who pulls for your greatness
And when you're being great
They are not over awed
Or jealous
Because they want to see you succeed even more than you do
That's a true friend
And if you fall
They fall with you
And when you stand back up
They stand back up with you
And maybe that's real love.

To a slave in the plantations of Southern America
Deep in the shackles of chattel slavery
At the peak of the period of the triangular slave trade
If you whispered in their ear that one day this would all be over
Only the most hopeful would believe
The rest would think it impossible
A black person in Jim Crow America
Colonial Africa
Apartheid Africa
Deep in the heart of these brutal times
If you whispered in their ear
One day this will all be over
Only the most courageous would believe
A Jewish child in Nazi Germany
A child in London listening to the whistles of the descending Nazi bombs
Whilst hiding in the bunker
Fearful
If you told them one day it would all be over
They might have believed
Only because they value the word of their loving parents
Their guardians
But one day
An over arching rhetoric comes along
A decisive moment
A twist in the tale
Even these brutal warlords
I've heard of one such during a war in Eastern Europe

He so terrorised his enemies that in the end
Even the mention of his name drew morbid fear into the minds of those who had faced and heard of his brutality
The civilian casualties of war
Such that when he was taken to the International Court of Justice
In his later years charged for war crimes
The victims were even scared to go into the courtroom
So much had his menace colonised their imagination
But by then he was old
And when they stepped in
They were shocked to see this frail old man
Unrepentant
But frail and old
The giant monster in their mind just but a little decaying husk
And there it is
So it is
In the end
In the end
I say darkness loses
It just has to give way to the light
When the light shines the darkness disappears
The light is its master

Not the other way round
But whilst you are in the dark
You can't see your way
A way

And fear abounds
Except for those who carry their own light within
A torch that illuminates the way
But when you come out of the cave
Out of the darkness
Or the sun's irrepressible light comes in
The darkness will
Will
And always will give way
So, when things seem impossible
And the agents of darkness seem insurmountable
All that needs to happen is for the good to remain good
Stay the course
Be smart and evolve
Though the dark ones may encase themselves in thick layers of armour to shield the light from coming in
In the end
Once you breach that shield
The whole edifice collapses
But the good must remain good
And know that the master of all in this plain is time
So, when you mind is boggled by the acts of evil ones
Do not be dismayed
However
Be emboldened
For they give you purpose
They say to you
Will you discover your greatness?
So, all the wars shall end one day

There will be peace on earth
One day.

I spoke to a man
A man who looks after orphans
Orphans and the abandoned
Abandoned and economically deprived children in his country
An African country suffering the ills all African countries suffer
All these ills we know of
Hundreds of these children
He has committed his life to
Scraping to provide them with food and shelter
An education
Yet the most profound thing he said was
When you restore hope
When you restore love
To a child that had lost that hope and love
That is a good thing
And he believed God saw that
How incredible to be a man
Who all he wants to do is restore hope and love
To those who have lost it
Or have none at all
More so
These poor young souls
God bless these beautiful hearts
Floating in our midst
They tip the balance
The cosmic balance against all that is dark here
Such that maybe the Gods who judge our stupidity
Keep giving us one more chance.

Young man
How can you sing?
Sing so beautifully
It brings tears to the eyes
Uncontrollable tears
Every time
Perhaps a piece of heaven you've brought with you
To herald a new dawn.

Where I thought there was an impasse
No way round
What could she possibly say
All logic and reason couldn't see a way
My logic and reason
What could she possibly say to turn this around
I can't possibly see any other answer
But I then was to discover
That love does truly find a way
It's not glib or facile
Or trite
An overused aphorism
It is true to say
Love finds a way
Be willing to listen and compromise
Turns out the answer and the truth
Lay somewhere between the both of us
Between our ability to effectively communicate.

I never knew I could love this much
I knew I could love
But not this much
Constantly growing
Constantly expanding
An unstoppable chain reaction
Continual explosions
Continuous explosions
Birthing new love
New love
New love.

Righteous anger
Righteous anger
Righteous anger
Is there such a thing?
Or is there only anger?

The greatest source of everything
Is nothing.

Mean what you say
And say what you mean
Otherwise, you are just practicing duplicity
And have a forked tongue
But also say and mean good things
Otherwise, it's all for nothing
And certainly destructive
Our spoken and written words
Are how we channel
Good and bad
Positive and negative
Love and hateful energy into our realm.

Turns out in the end
That they were always right
Throughout all of our time
That gratitude
Gratitude is the ultimate practice
Gratitude in all circumstances
At all times
Under all the burdens
And all the joys
Gratitude
Gratitude
Gratitude always
That's the highest realisation.

The most arduous challenge I had today
How to finish this 8oz burger
Placed in front of me by the most attentive of waiters
Not one
Not two
But three of them
Had come unbeknownst to each other to ask if I wanted to order my drink
Of course I had told their first colleague
So here I am
The only black skinned man or person in sight
In this lovely establishment
On this sunny day
Facing out into the sea
With the cliffs as a backdrop
On these Shetland Islands
I had had a moment of crisis
A child from colonial Africa
I'm the only black person in here
But Raleigh
We are all human beings
How many times have you written that
Yet the paranoia I had to settle
The paranoia infused in our minds by the certain media
Certain political affiliations
Certain perspectives
And yet calm I became
For I am finding myself

And in so many ways I am convinced of the beauty of it all
The beauty of everyone
So back to this burger
These chunky chips
Good luck with that said the lovely elderly gentleman sat opposite me with his lovely lady
I quipped back
I think I need two stomachs for this
I am more comfortable nowadays with this polite unscripted chit chat with strangers
I have come out of my shell
Yet when they arrived
Of course I had Judged them
That nasty little voice
That sees an old white man and expects the worst
How wrong I was in the end
For once the meal was done
And he congratulated me on my accomplishment
We all then had the most beautiful human exchange
I have ever had with strangers
Maybe things are changing
Maybe I am changing
For it was never the world out there to change
It was the world in here
Yet the dilemma of this burger

More than two people could eat
Could feed five children in Kibera
This mighty succulent burger I have devoured

With massive chunky chips
In this beautiful place
This lone black man
In a sea of white people
Thank you Nelson
Thank you Malcolm
Thank you Martin
Thank you Rosa
Thank you James Baldwin
Thank you all
You gave me this moment
As I shed tears
Trying to hide them from onlookers
I wonder
Am I too emotional?
There is so much to contemplate though
So much to aggregate
So I'll give myself a pass
I'm sensitive
An empath
Yet war rages in places in the world
Others starve
That man just stabbed those people and children in France
I was asked to attend a protest against a Neo Nazi group I can't attend
There are actually neo Nazis in the world
Follow Hitler's ideology
Proudly
Boldly and openly

Yet
Today I have never felt more at peace in my entire existence
In love with my existence
Existing
An energy healer I had seen in the morning
She massages the body but it's also holistic
Meaning the physical body and elements that go beyond the physical
Something had told me that would be the result today
And before the session she asked me to pick a card from her bag
Any card
They all seemed to say relevant things I would want
One would want
Confidence and the like
But I picked self love
And as I write this ode
In this moment
For someone who has had issues with self esteem
Self confidence
Self appreciation

For longer in my life than one would want
Loving the world
Loving life
Suicidal thinking
For the greater part of my existence
The fact that I've felt the love I've felt today
For life

Existence
And myself
All one can in the end say
Is yes, we are here
In the so-called flesh
But we are also everywhere
Leading to the same conclusion
Leading to the same conclusion
As always.

I have such a hankering to write the most beautiful poem
Which encapsulates everything about life
In one poem
Talk about Lauryn Hill
And 90s r'n'b which was so moving
Captured my youth
The sounds of which
Send my soul into a tailspin of nostalgia when I hear them
Talk about Motown
A golden era of music
About Whitney Houston
The inimitable Bob Marley
Bob
An extraordinaire
Only matched by the one and only
Michael Jackson
The Smooth Criminal
Thriller
Phil Collins
Whitney sang of the greatest love of all
Bob sang no woman no cry
Michael sang the earth song
And the man in the mirror
Phil saw your true colours shining
Then I realise I could never write the most beautiful poem
It's already been written
By all of us

For no one person's vision of the truth of it all
Can surpass or surmount
The collective observations
Emotions
Sentiments
Expressions of the soul
Of the billions of souls
That have come and gone
So then now I can rest easily
I see it's not down to me
It's not up to just me
I can't do it alone
Could never have
Maybe that's why I went mad
The madness of life drove me mad
I took the whole burden into my shoulders
Into my mind
Into my heart
It was reflexive but it was naïve
So, I can be forgiven for not knowing
I can forgive myself for thinking it was up to and down to me
It was and is always up to and down to all of us.

Tulsa
Emmett
Aboriginals
Native Americans
Tales of dastardly deeds
George Floyd
The human story.

In the thicket
Of existence.

Mr Baldwin
How could you be so calm and collected?
Acerbic yet again calm
Critical
Dextrous in the moment
Having to articulate against their best thinkers
Those who held the opposite view
To be so intelligent
Articulate
Knowledgeable
Melodious
Mellifluous
As though you were singing a song
Reciting a poem
Pre prepared and rehearsed
A speech
But yet I see
It was the authenticity of your gift
To describe what you see
Saw
And meet it with the highest expression of what it is to be human
Not hatred or anger
But the deepest understanding
Reflection and longing
For what could be better
And more
Deconstruct the edifice of supremacy and hatred whilst looking at it in it's line of sight.

And then when you thought
The main thing was getting to the end of the tunnel
The end of your travails
Or the travails of that particular moment
You realise
No
There is more tunnel
There are more travails
Then the insight becomes
Mastering always pursuing the light
Knowing you're always in a tunnel
Or even more so
Being the light
Then the tunnel becomes irrelevant.

Turns out the only way to truly win Is to stop fighting.

So, adults
Are just children who grew up
Then forced to face the challenges of the world
The ravages of the world
Yet still children they remain
But in bigger bodies
With more responsibilities
And fate in their own hands
Yet still children they remain
And what do they know?
How tragic
How amazing
How incredible
To all of a sudden be thrust
Infront of the raging lion that is life at times
That little frightened boy and girl
Curled up inside constantly wanting to turn away
Or worse yet
Constantly trying to prove themselves
Trying to survive
Survive the raging lion.

Until you choose to love someone
That means love them despite their flaws
That means your disagreements with them
You're not yet in love
Your love is conditional
On the condition that they treat you a certain way
Or are a certain way
Spoil you
And all that
But real love begins when you go past the superficial enjoyment
And deal with their shortcomings
For you too have short comings
We are all human
Then the journey of true love begins
That's why of course the only trick then
Is to make sure you are with someone who has an equal commitment to you
Feels as strongly for you
That way your commitment
Your choice doesn't become one-sided
Because that kind of one-sided commitment
One sided choice
Leads to places not all that enjoyable.

We are all perishables
To be consumed by mother earth
Just like the fruits and vegetables we eat
To return to the energy cycle
The energetic realm.

To teach real discipline
True discipline
True principles
You don't deny someone access to a thing
You give them access to the thing
Then teach them why they shouldn't access it
Or partake in a particular behaviour
Give them choice
Give them autonomy
Empower them
Let them be the master over their impulses
Then you've taught them real discipline
Then they are truly disciplined
Just like the martial artists trained in all the lethality of their discipline
The deadliest techniques
But is disciplined not to use them
A master of their impulses
That's true discipline
Not imposition of will
As with a child
Teach them to choose
Choose the right thing
Not teach them fear
Or force them
Then that's just the world we know.

It would be funny
If it wasn't so dangerous
So impactful
After all the hypothetical conjecture
The phenomenon is really real
Feels for all intents and purposes truly real
Totally and completely immersive.

I have just listened to a man say
Africa civilised Europe not once
But twice
First it was the Egyptians
Who taught the Greeks
Who then taught the Romans
Then a dark age befell Europe for five hundred years
Then it was the Moors again of Africa
Went to Spain
A history that's of course been erased
And another process of so called civilisation
Whether it's true or not
Who knows
Who cares
That's not how the world looks like today
I was raised by society to think I was inferior
Tacitly and more openly
By the European imposing civilisations
How did the so called civiliser find themselves here then?
In any case
I really don't care about all that now
White people did this
Black people are like that
All I care about now is what world I am creating for my children
What future
This history
This present
This Dichotic Dilemma

I want it to matter no more
And only matter in terms of deepening our realisation
of humanity
Of existence
All these other things
Other than these things.

I heard a lady say
She was a wise lady
An African lady
An African wise lady
And they asked her
As she was eating food with her hands
Why do Africans eat food with their hands?
She said
It accentuates the process of eating food
The taste
The experience
Your hands are connected to your brain
Of course
And when you touch the food
It tells the brain about the texture
The characteristics of the food you are about to eat
And prepares the brain
The receptors
Your mouth
Your taste buds
Your salivary glands for the food
So not so primitive and uncivilised after all
And yet they came and said
Look at you
You savage beast
Use these man made implements
A fork
A knife
A spoon
For thusly you shall be civilised

Casting the spell of their superiority
And instilling a sense if inferiority in those they had conquered
Yet it seems eating with your hands is absolutely fine after all
Implies no lack of humanity or civility
So, I will eat with my hands
As I always have
And a folk, knife and a spoon
For I want to be in tune with all that is.

The continuous story of human existence
Truly fascinating
Today I met a man
A man from my land
A man before my time
A man ahead of my time
Incredible
His story was truly fascinating
Illuminating
When the truth becomes even more true
And reality even more real
And gripping
What you thought was
Wasn't quite
And what was
Was even more astounding
Oh yes
His story started during the unrest of the independence struggle
Yet he went on to live a most remarkable and successful life
Though our paths crossed only for a moment
You see that the human spirit was always soaring even back then
When you would have thought it was more subdued
Or had more reason to be so
Hope
Hope
Hope.

Poetry
The opening to expand the limits
The limits of thinking and feeling
Just like hope.

I think to myself
What is the point of sending probes to deep space?
What is the point of contemplating life beyond earth?
Outside of the gravitational pull that binds us here
We don't even get along here
Where its bountiful
At least the environment is largely hospitable
Food and water plentiful
The atmosphere kind
Reliable seasons
Habitable climates
A continuous source of nourishment provided by mother Earth
Allows us to be stupid and foolish
Like spoilt rich kids who can live life with reckless abandon
Knowing there is more where that came from
It's without real consequence
But out there in space
Where its dark and cold
Void
Unbreathable
Unknown
What chance do we have?
Shouldn't we learn to walk first?

That is understand the meaning of life
Why we are here together
Before we run
Run into space
Maybe that's why this alien life we search for hides itself from us
Why would they bother
What silly beasts they must say
What silly creatures
Why waste our time
If we told them what we knew
Their civilisation would end in an instant
Like a toddler given a loaded gun in a kindergarten playground
What wise being would do that?
Space
I say forget it
Not till the utter foolishness stops
Then maybe we can start
Just as the whites in America looked up in wonder as the first rockets to space were launched
The blacks thought only of their despair
As a toddler
With a loaded gun
And for these satellites in California and elsewhere
SETI
They will never reveal themselves to us
Not as we are
We will never find them
We are beyond primitive and so is our technology

How do I know?
I just know
And if I was them
I would never reveal myself to this humanity
Not as we are.

In a taxi I was
Being ferried from A to B
The radio on
Quietly conditioning us
For a play was on through the radio
Could have been radio two
Or four
I didn't quite see
The BBC
And a man says in the play being broadcast on the radio
"With this current generation being the way they are
How are we going to build new Empires?"
New Empires I thought
New Empires?
Who wants to build new Empires?
Like the old Empires
Of pillage, rape and ruin
Greed and destruction
Death and disease
Who wants to build that?
How is that on the radio?
Who still thinks that way?
The world needs more rich people
Not more conquered people
The world needs more comfortable people
We should be lifting people out of poverty
A sustainable, cooperative, comfortable world
Empire?
Empire?

What dinosaurs are these?
How does one aspire for such things?
Aspire for Barbarism
And yet I saw this in my younger days
As a young man
This baffling duality of reality
And of course I called it
The Dichotic Dilemma
For what a Dichotomy
The world I and I'm sure many dream of
And the world others dream of too
Of conquest and dominance
Not peace and love
That's the dilemma of existence
So, in the end
One can only do
What one can do
And that's it
Yes it was supposedly a play
But there is no smoke without fire

And healthy caution is good caution
More so an appropriate steering of human philosophy.

Concentric levels of perception.

The innocence of children
Should always be our guide.

In the end
It's not really about better politics
Or who's politics is better
Capitalists
Or Socialists
Liberals and the rest
They'll always argue their side
Really in the end
It's about better humans
That's all there is to it
For the history books tell the story clearly
Constantly fighting over ideas
Which are better
Which are worse
Religion
Superiority
Control of resources
The only answer
Is better humans
Nothing less
Storied philosophers, moralists and ethical thinkers
are as old as written history
Yet we are still here
So better human
Failing that
It seems
It'll only be more of the same
Or even yet
A setting of the sun on us.

What diseased thinking
To think you should
Or can own other human beings
Are superior to them
These divine creatures
This divine existence
From where we come
Who knows
To where we go
Who knows
And you here
Meek and small
See yourself that great
What diseased thinking.

So, earth is the place where evil can thrive
And it does thrive
Hence why it seems at times
The most evil
Seem to get away with it all
Yet the good must always persist
Even as they throw their bodies
Their very flesh
Infront of tanks
Pushing always for a better tomorrow
Hope.

So, the Afro centrists
Those so called to have black consciousness
They like to say
We were Kings in the past
We were not this
This that so many think we are
This negative story that's been told
This caricature
This thing that has been socially
Colonially
Economically
And brutally engineered
At least some of it
Some elements searching for identity
Re
Membering
Re
Assembling
Re
Ascending
To a higher sense of self
As we all must
Discover the highest sense of ourselves
This is all I wish.

Does Magic exist?
Magic being possibility beyond the perceptibly possible
Occurrences
Abilities
Transformation
Beyond the everyday and mundane
That's why some people don't believe in God
In miracles
They see a cold dark world
A cold dark uncaring Universe
Just fixed objects
Fixed immovable objects and horrible fates
Powers beyond their mortal ability to shift and change
So, does Magic exist?
Does God exist?
Yes.

It seems we are all born into a perspective
Elucidation
Elucidation
Elucidation.

A treatise
On healthy scepticism
To be a healthy sceptic
Is actually to be objective
Yet subjective concomitantly
To be a healthy sceptic
Is to believe anything is possible
Whilst staying grounded in your perceptions
For the inverse is to get lost
In the surging winds of all that's possible
And all these varying perspectives
There are just so many
There is just so much
And you certainly don't want to get trapped
In the trap of absolutism
That's the right, wrong paradigm
The bane of human existence
So, the healthy sceptic
Stands right in the head winds
Of all these ideas
Opinions
Beliefs
And filters through
Not completely accepting
Not completely denying

But being
Being a conduit to try and work out
As much as we can work out
What the totality of the truth is
What is the totality of our truth
What is the totality of the truth we see
We all see
We can see with the limitations and the capabilities of our faculties
In our multifarious perspectives.

You have to set the highest standard
But be understanding
Of the lowest parameters
The lowest manifestations
And machinations.

The irony
Of a land so bountiful and beautiful
To draw envy and desire
Such that those that occupy it are content
And those that covet it
It's bounty
 Are insatiable
And so became the story
Yet
It is the story
The broadest story
And to narrow it in focus
Perhaps too reductionist
To limit the scope
And the range of observation
Of course
Not the best path to tread.

Imagine inheriting an inferiority complex
A spiritual inferiority complex
On a mass scale
Or is it socially conditioned?
Or is Life ultimately a personal struggle?
A lonely, contained, individual battle
In a wider context
It's even more confusing
When everything is true.

Days and days
And days
I sat
With seemingly no meaning
Days upon days
Like years
Like lifetimes
Full of mundanity and boredom
Days and days
Then all at once
Like a dam bursting
Under the pressure of the flood waters
Opportunities in life started gushing out
The Upward turn
Then to realise in some ways
They were always there
And in other ways
God just wants you to soak it all in
Soak in the mundanity
The boredom
Just be an existing thing
A thing in existence
Then you are truly
Just existing
Being
Then when you master just being
Well
You can truly be.

You are alive.

Facts
Facts
Facts
Meaningless facts
Of course we can use them to create
But we can also use them
To create weapons
Weaponise them
For with the same facts
You can tell different stories
Infer different meanings
So, do the facts
The stats
The statistics
Reflect truth
Or reflect who you are
Hence
Is there even such a thing as a fact?

A miscrable person
Spreads misery
Hence
Your job is to make yourself as happy as possible
But
Yet
Knowing
There are billions of other human beings
And everything else
Whilst fulfilling on the good that you can bring.

Love is a gravity
And we are like cosmic bodies
Rather
We are cosmic bodies.

The dilemma
The competition
The schism
The merits
And demerits
Of collective accumulation
Against
Individual accumulation
Being first
Or having no concept of first
Getting the most
Or all getting.

I know now
What they mean
When they say someone touched your heart
Touched your soul
For I felt it today
Thank you Mam
I think she was an angel
Hope.

Hope is defined as a feeling of expectation and desire for a particular thing to happen on the Google search engine results. The receptacle of all instantaneous knowledge in the Twenty first century. The amalgam of almost all of Humanity's collected knowledge a few punches of a key board away. Of course and all else that comes with a quick Google search. The expression of what we call the human condition. What I call the Dichotic Dilemma of course.

Yes, so hope. A feeling of expectation and desire for a particular thing to happen. Hence, on this basis one can see why it's often associated with wishing for a positive result. Especially in untoward circumstances.

The interesting thing about life, is we all live in our own personal little world where we can be in our own little hell or heavenly existence. At times not even consistent with the circumstances and change at different points in our life. This is why of course they talk about the power of the mind. Hence, this gives me hope that we can achieve the things I hope for by hoping everyone in our little bubbles of reality can see the beauty of reality. The reality we share together, because it's by believing in ugly things that we create an ugly world. If you see beauty within you will see it everywhere.

As I draw to a close, below is a poem my father penned. My father is more intelligent than I am so most times his poetry is too abstract for me and goes over my head. However, he did pen this one and I asked if I could steal his intellectual property and he obliged. However, in all seriousness, there was something deeply resonant about this piece. This man, strong, reliable, dependable, the man who has guided me along this whole path. Hence, I am honoured to share this piece of history associated with this book by having a poem my father penned in it and I hope the reader can resonate with the deep untouchable therein.

Zulu!!!
 Bayethe!!!

They call.
A salutation to the kings.
The trappings for which he adorns.
A white head dress to the fore of the head.
Favoured the emblem.
Zulu!!!
Bayethe.
The spirit he embodies.
From fields afar,
The aura, as in the motherland to envelope.
A recognition of one as such,
Persistent over time.
Zulu wa Bazulu.
Bayethe.

Bayethe, a powerful South African Zulu Royal salute of 'Hail. There is so much for me in here. Not only does it connect me as an African to a part of my historical story but more so as a Southern African because I am part Ndebele. The Ndebele being defectors from the Zulu Kingdom who fled inward and countered the Shona settling in the area now called Zimbabwe. I am also part Shona. So, an amalgam of a time of flux in Southern Africa just before the colonial conquest began which dramatically and inexorable changed the continent and in so many ways regrettably. So, this poem connects me to my history, a history that even Cambridge professors say doesn't exist when spouting supremacist ideology. So, this poem makes me hope for a world where, my story might not have mattered to some, hopefully in the future all our stories matter to all of us.

Hope

I hope for world peace. I hope for the end of war. The end of fighting. I hope for the transformation of Africa. On so many accounts and for all those who are poverty stricken there and cut off from the abundance of existence. Having to rely on the goodwill of others instead of their own ingenuity. Good Will which can be in short supply in this world of ours. This life of ours.

Of course, I hope for good will for everyone and in the end all I have is my hope. Hence, why I wrote a book titled Hope.

Some fight with guns, bombs, Machiavellian tactics, power, means of oppression, their trickery, perhaps their hatred. I am fighting with my hope.

I could do worse other than hoping for good things.

The battle is steep, can be steep. Inside and outside. A sage told me when I was lost and I thought with my ignorance and foolishness that I was here to save others. She said, you are here to save yourself and show others that you've done it. For years I didn't comprehend yet now I do. The demons within are plaguing enough before you think you can exorcise the demons without. If you set to exorcise the demons of others before you exorcise your own, you could just end up spreading the influence of your own demons. Cleanse yours first.

Hence, with that I hope the reader gets what the reader gets if there was anything to get from my humble point of observation. The only final thing to say being that, until humanity, perhaps even in it's totality is embroiled in a conversation. Not about politics, not about economics, not about gender, not about race, not about war, not about nationality, not about ethnicity, not about religious identity, not about cultural superiority, but instead embroiled itself in a conversation about love. Yes love. Love as a global topic. Not GDP but love. Not GNP but love. Not growth figures but love. Not political slogans but love. If ever that was to happen on this planet then maybe the things I have hoped for will happen. The things that have led me to write exhaustively to stress the point through the series of my writings. When humanity graduates to that level then it'll be a new humanity, a new planet, a new reality where my little children will see a different world.

Signed off

Twenty third June twenty twenty-three.

Seemingly I have concluded.

Hope you have enjoyed.

Hope.

I love the world. What a breathtaking opportunity to be individually and uniquely expressed.

www.ingramcontent.com/pod-product-compliance
Lightning Source LLC
LaVergne TN
LVHW091547060526
838200LV00036B/738